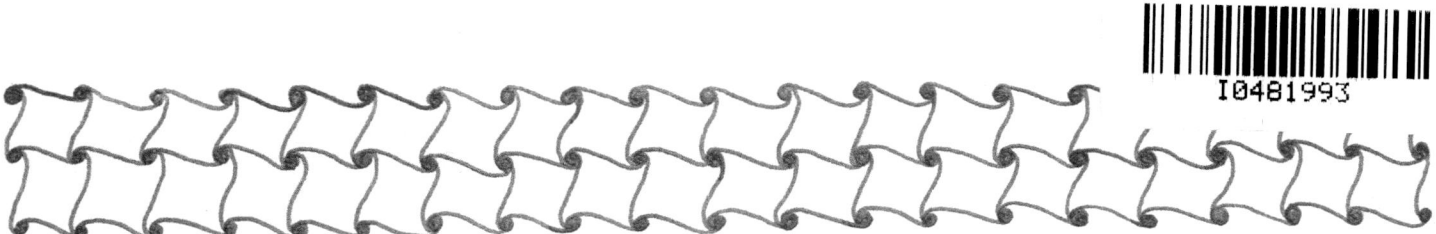

I0481993

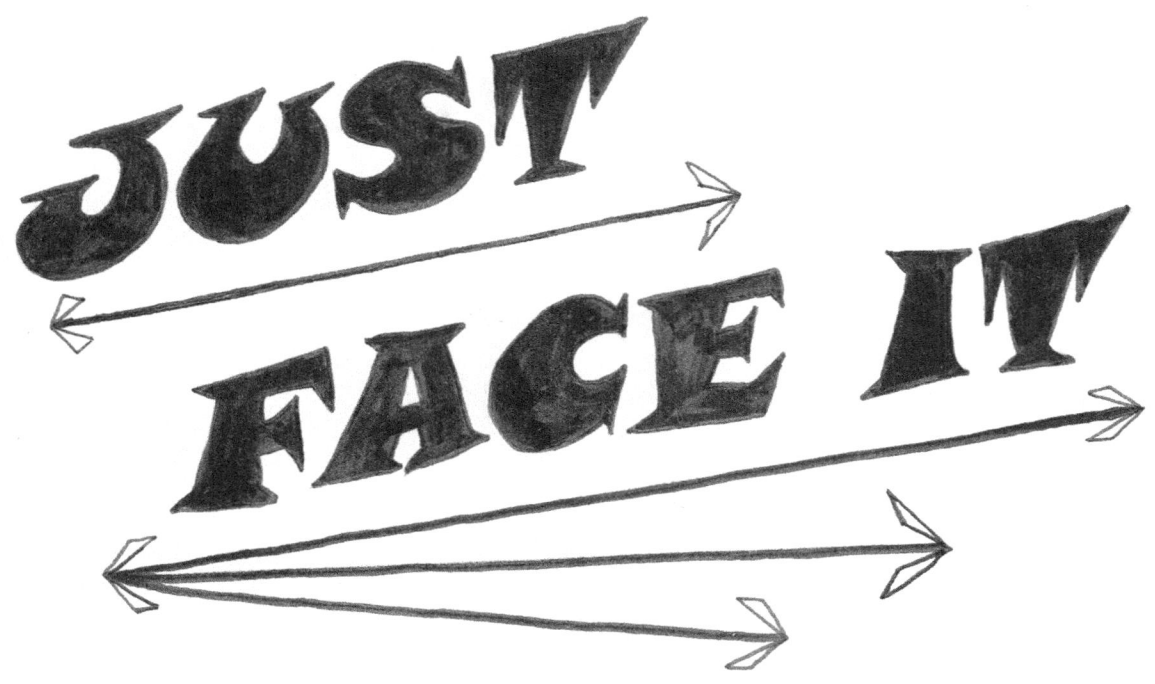

JUST FACE IT

An adult coloring book for real life emotions!

ISBN-13: 978-1981805549

ISBN-10: 1981805540

Dee Micenec

::::::: zendee4u@outlook.com :::::::

www.facebook.com/profile.php?id=100011820423254

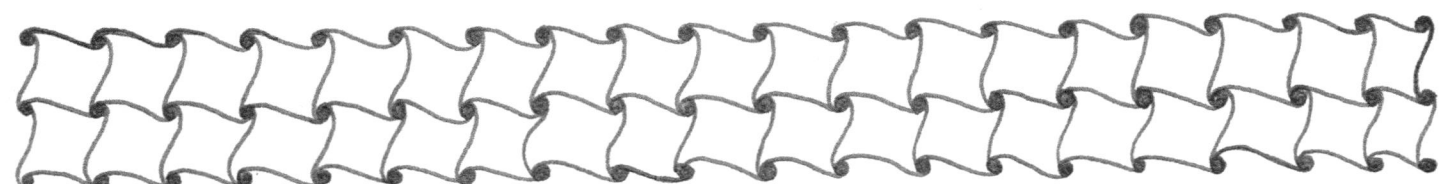

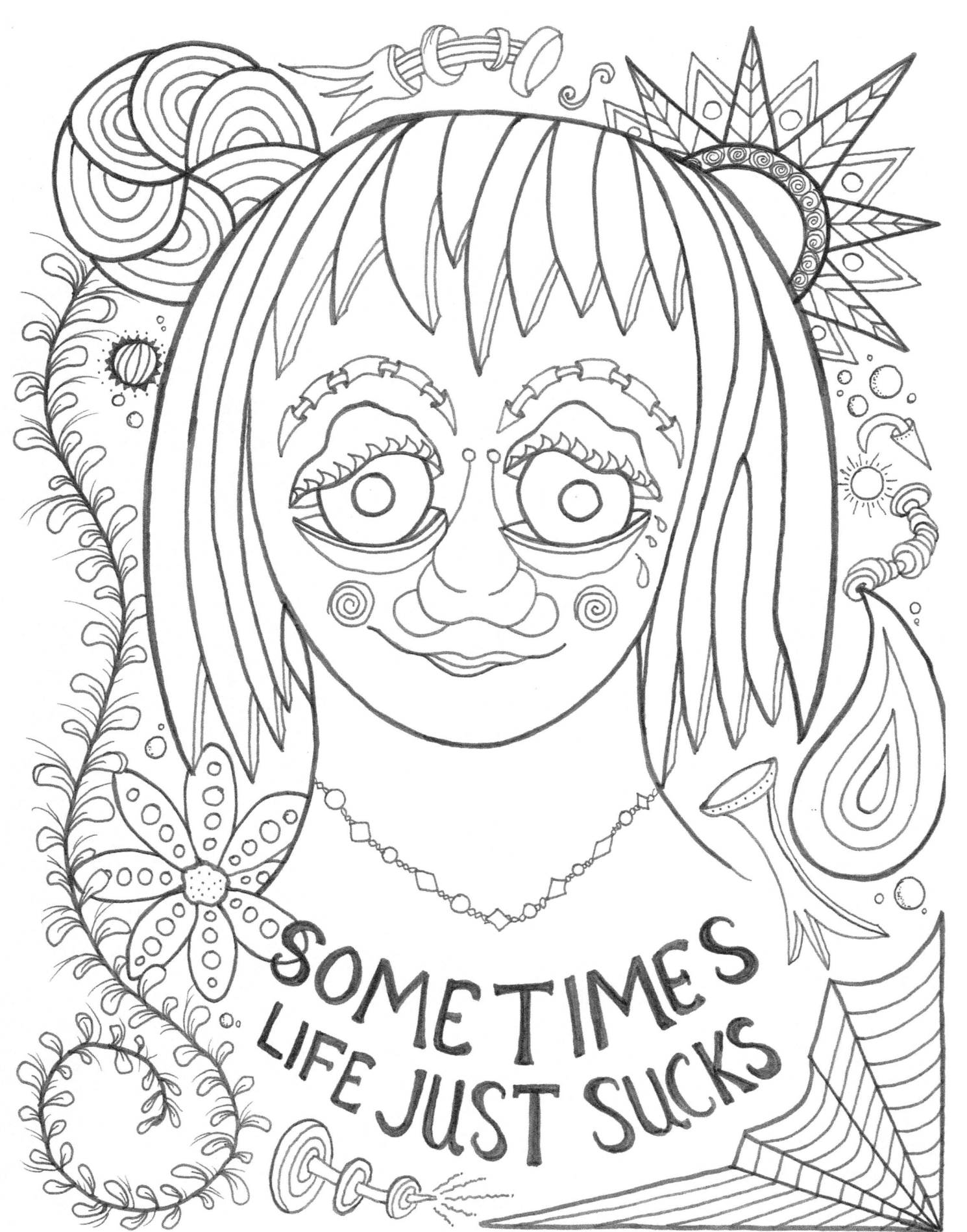

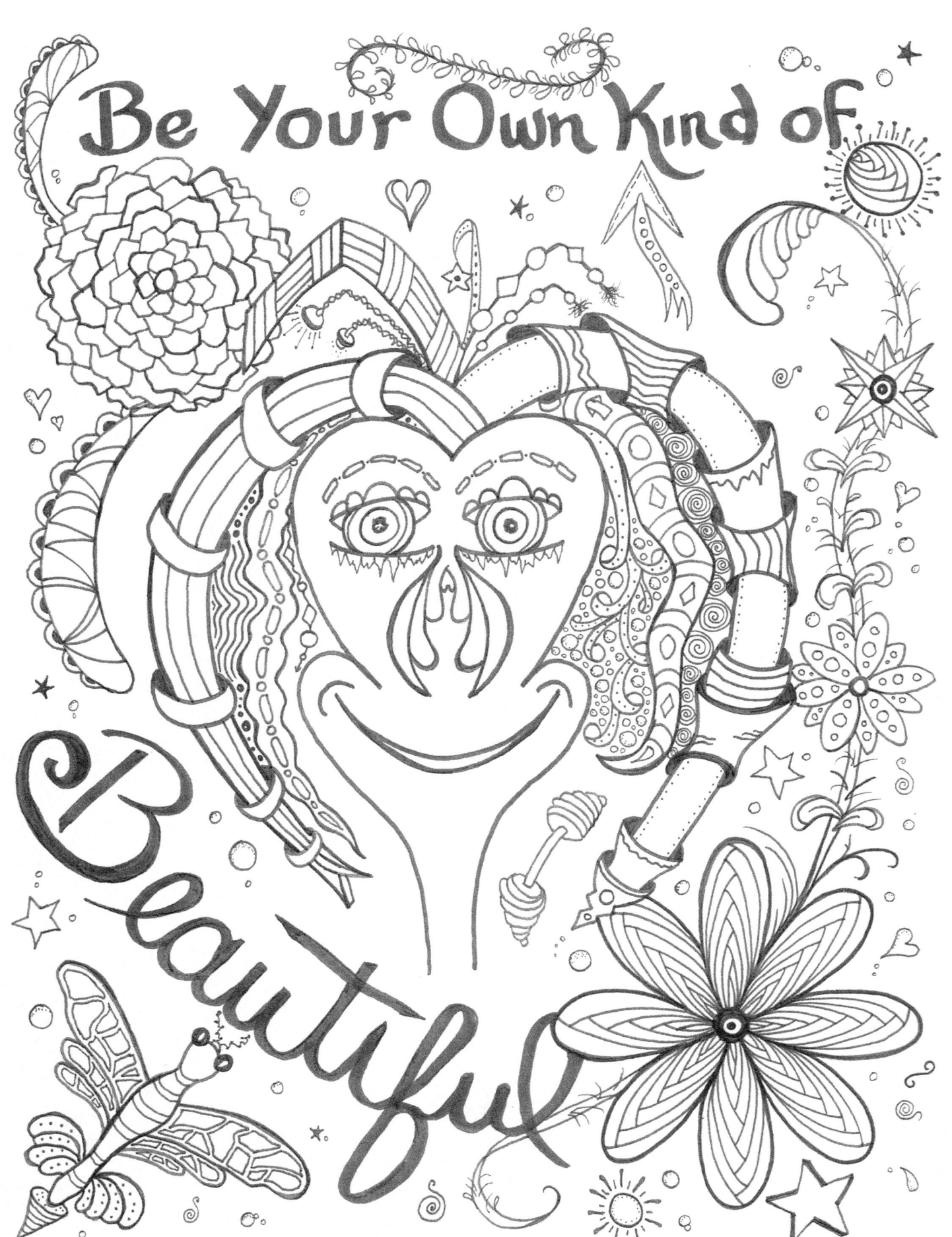

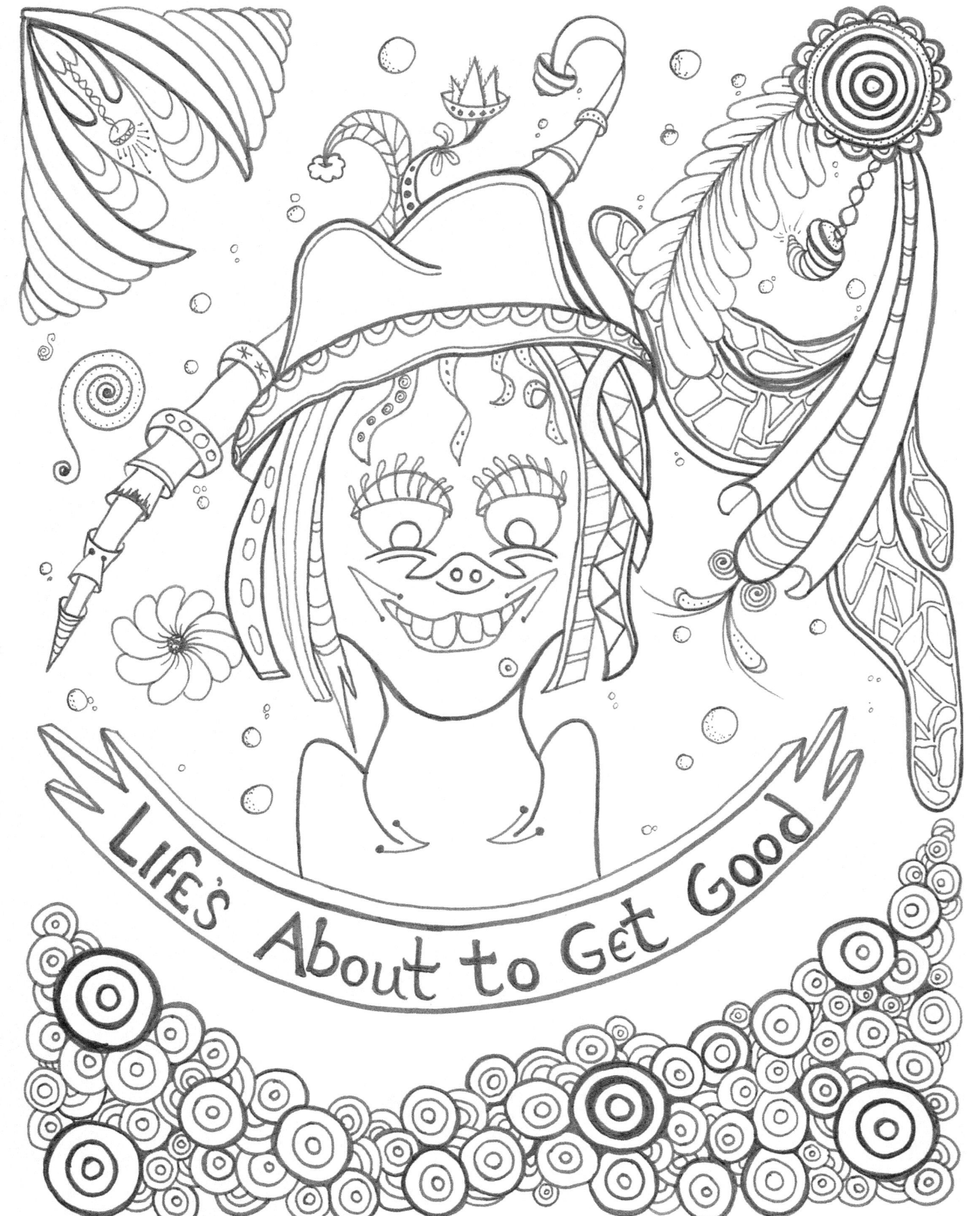

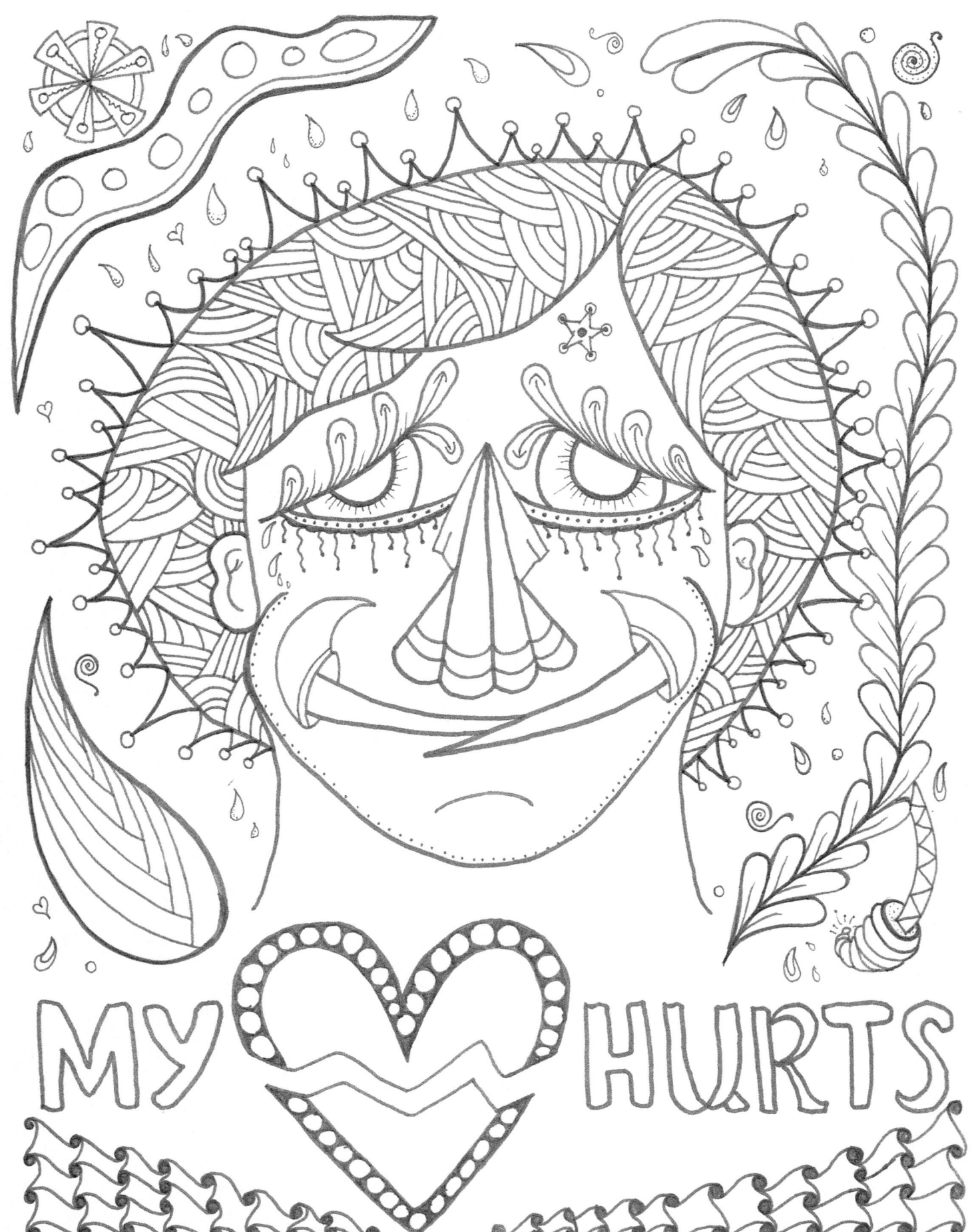

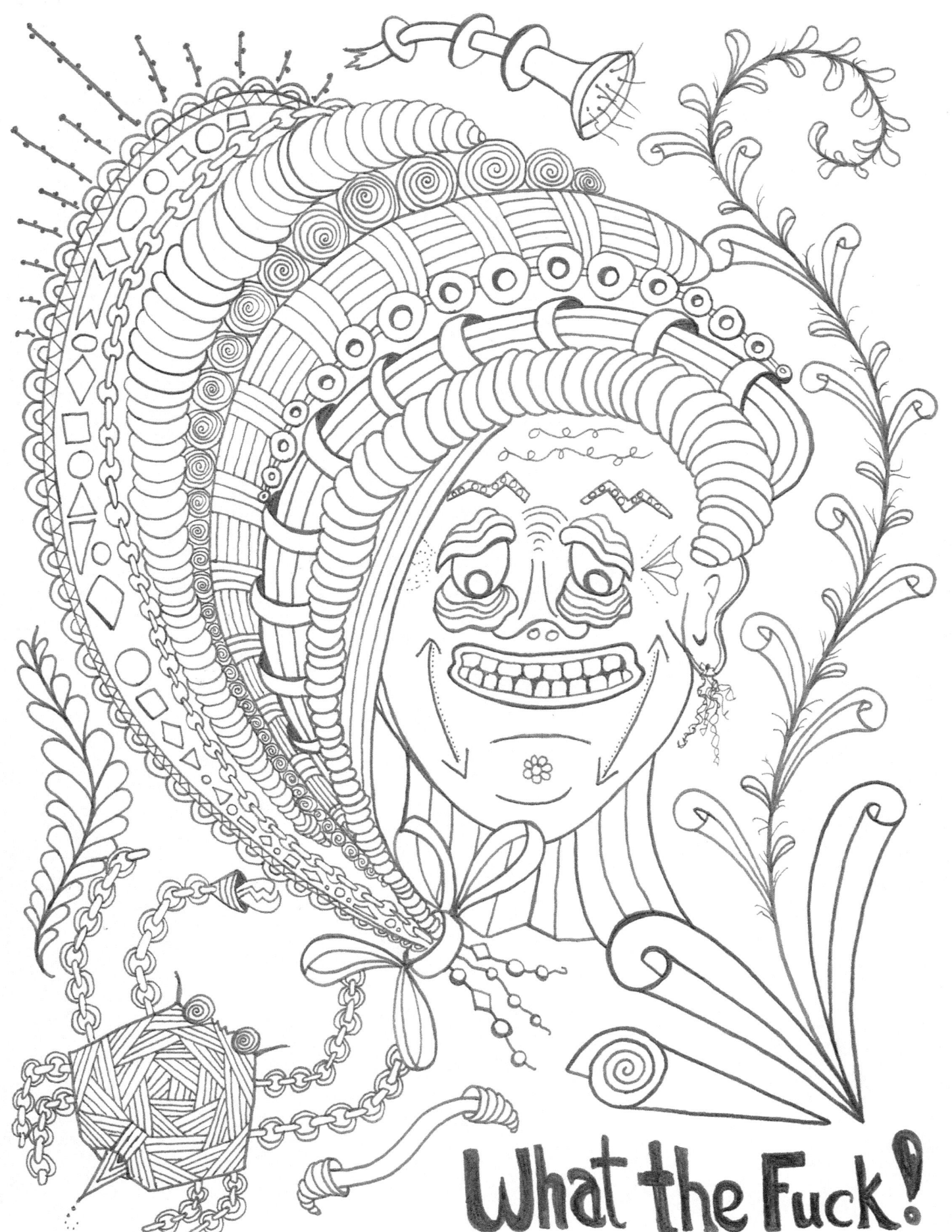

What the Fuck!

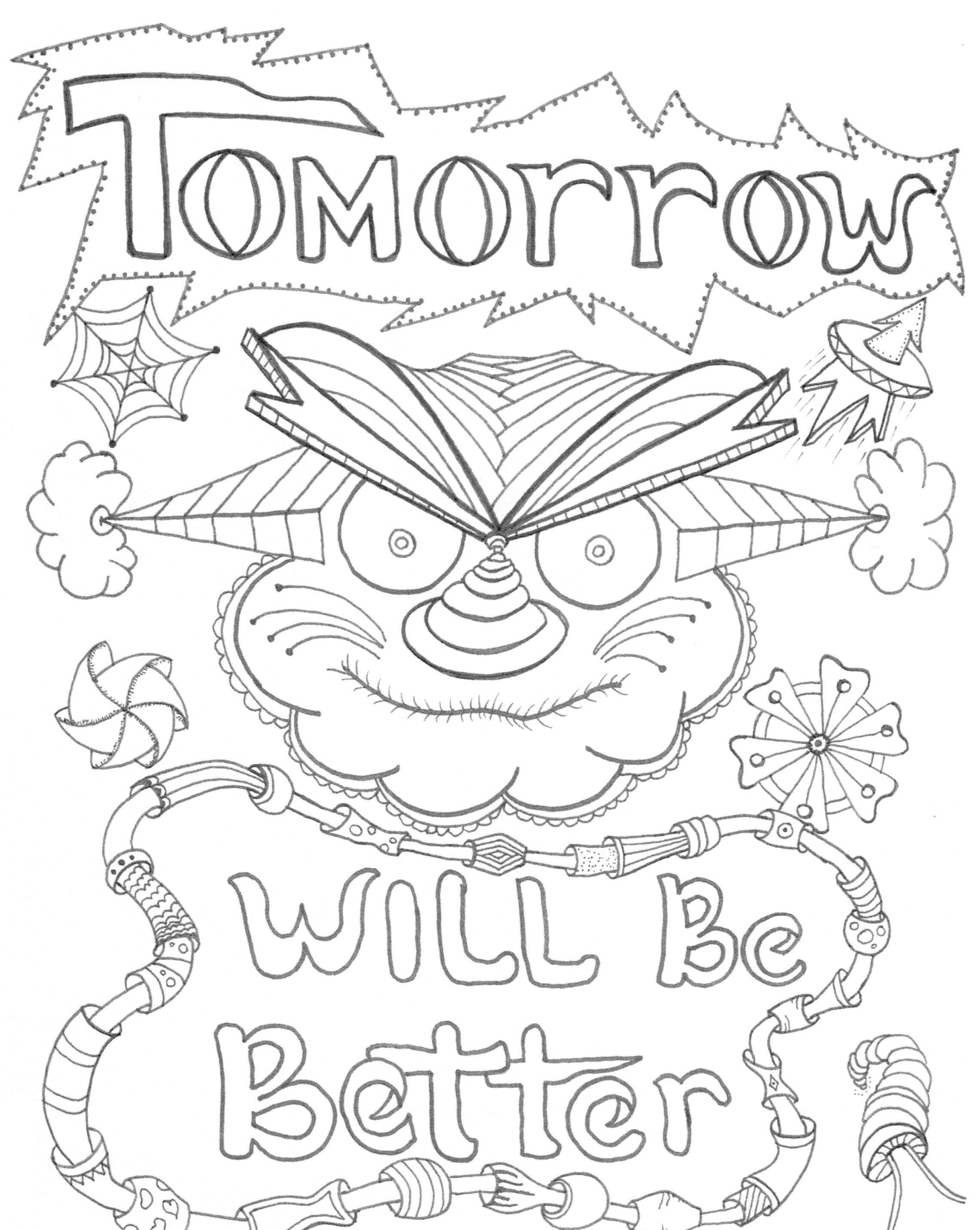

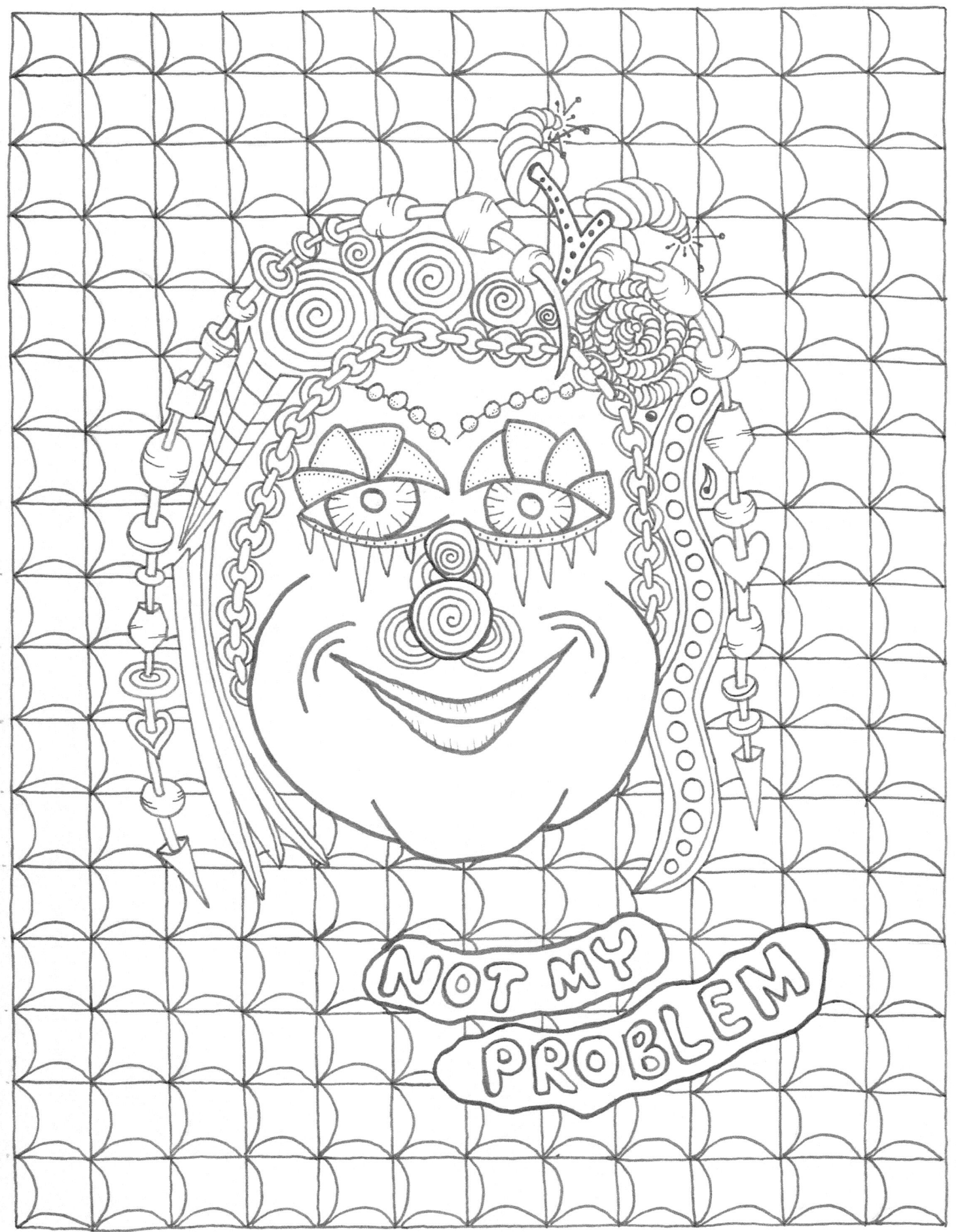

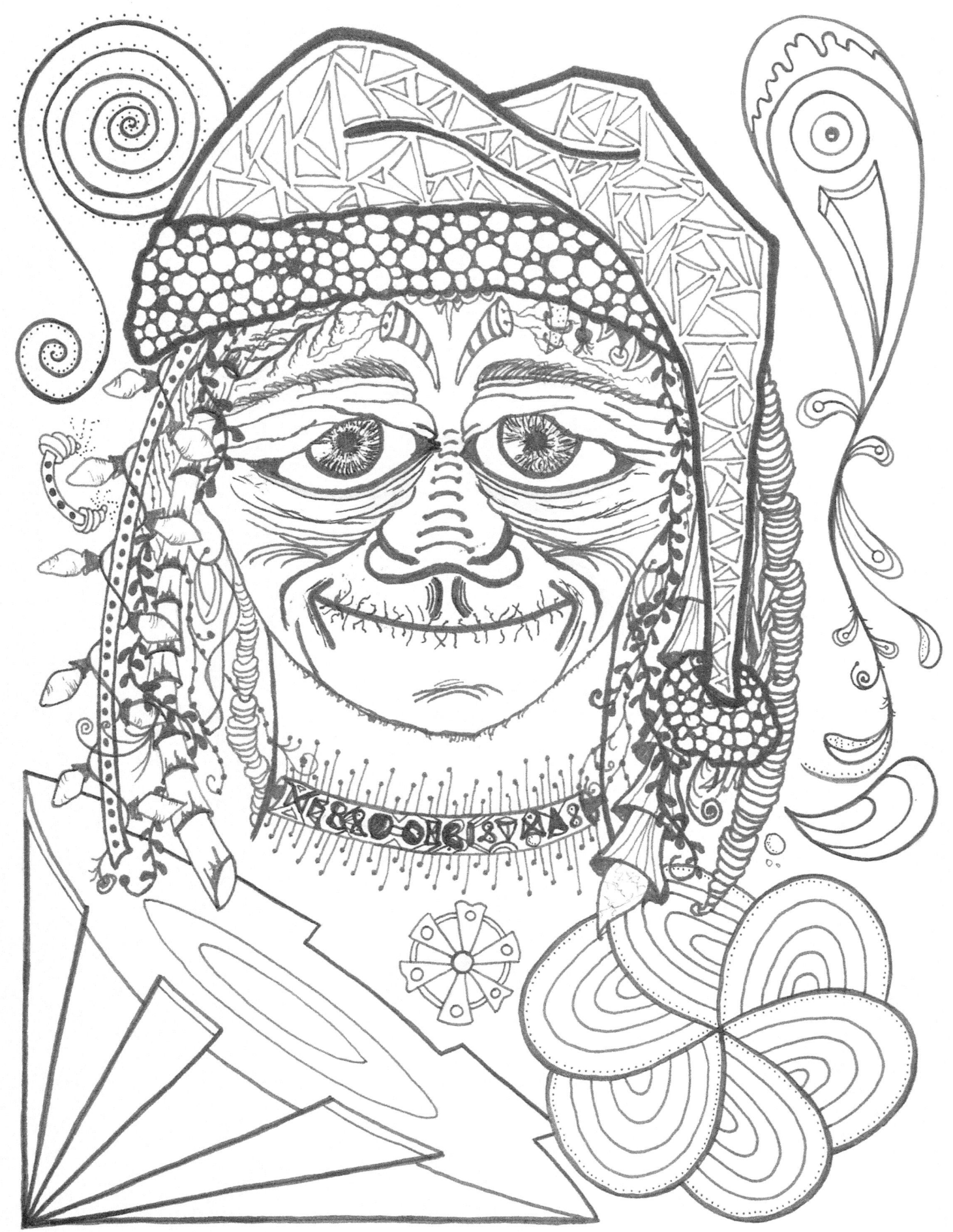

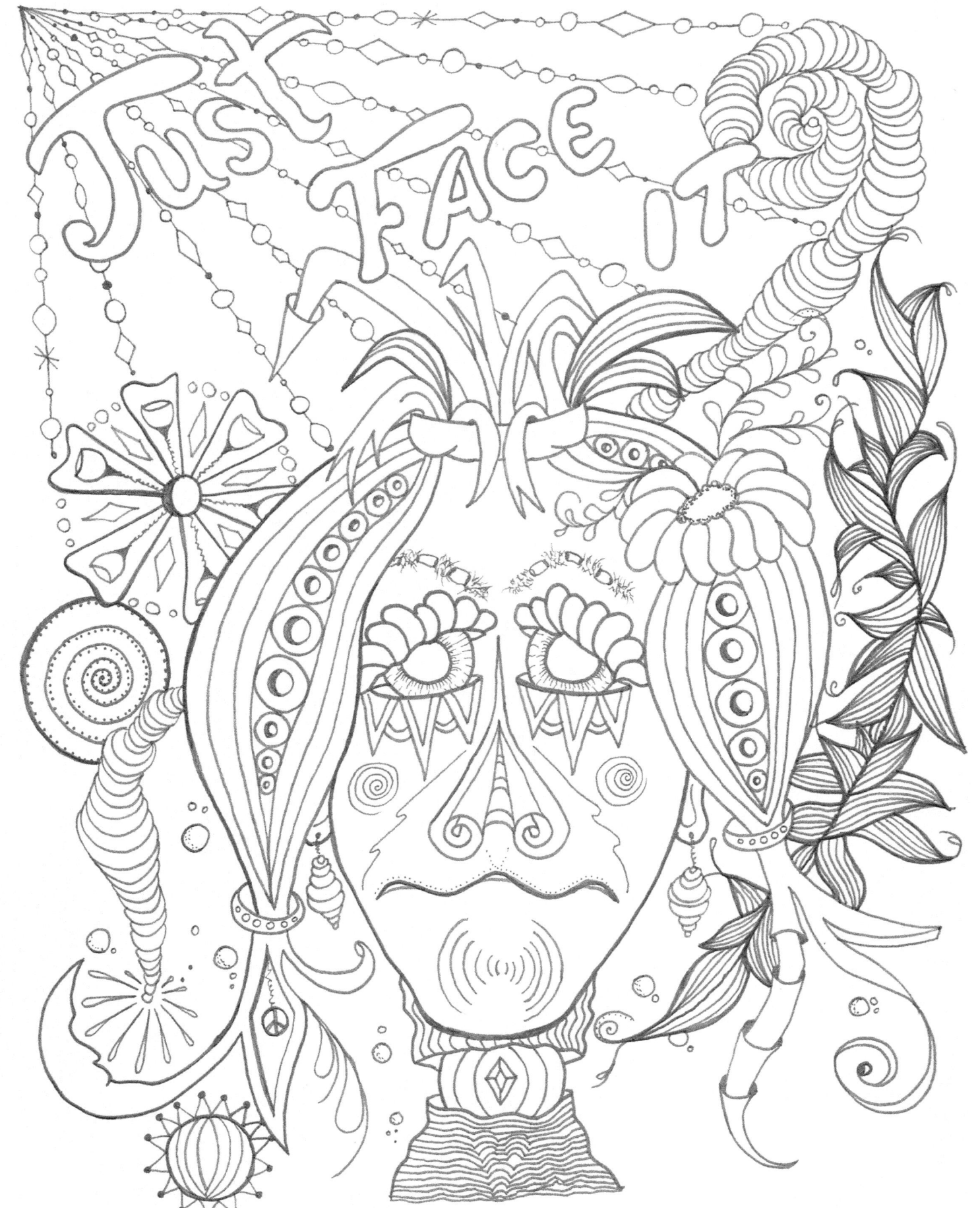

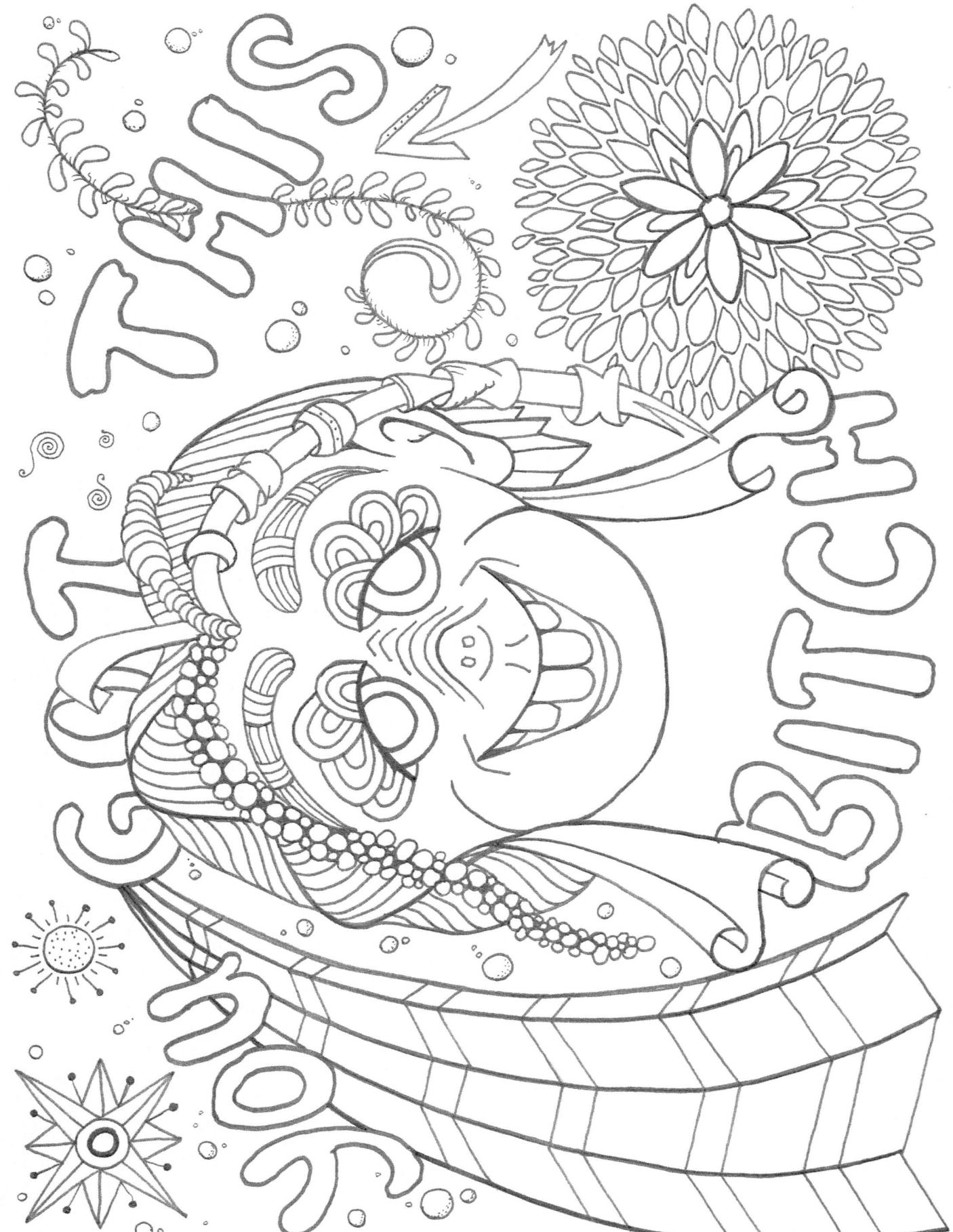

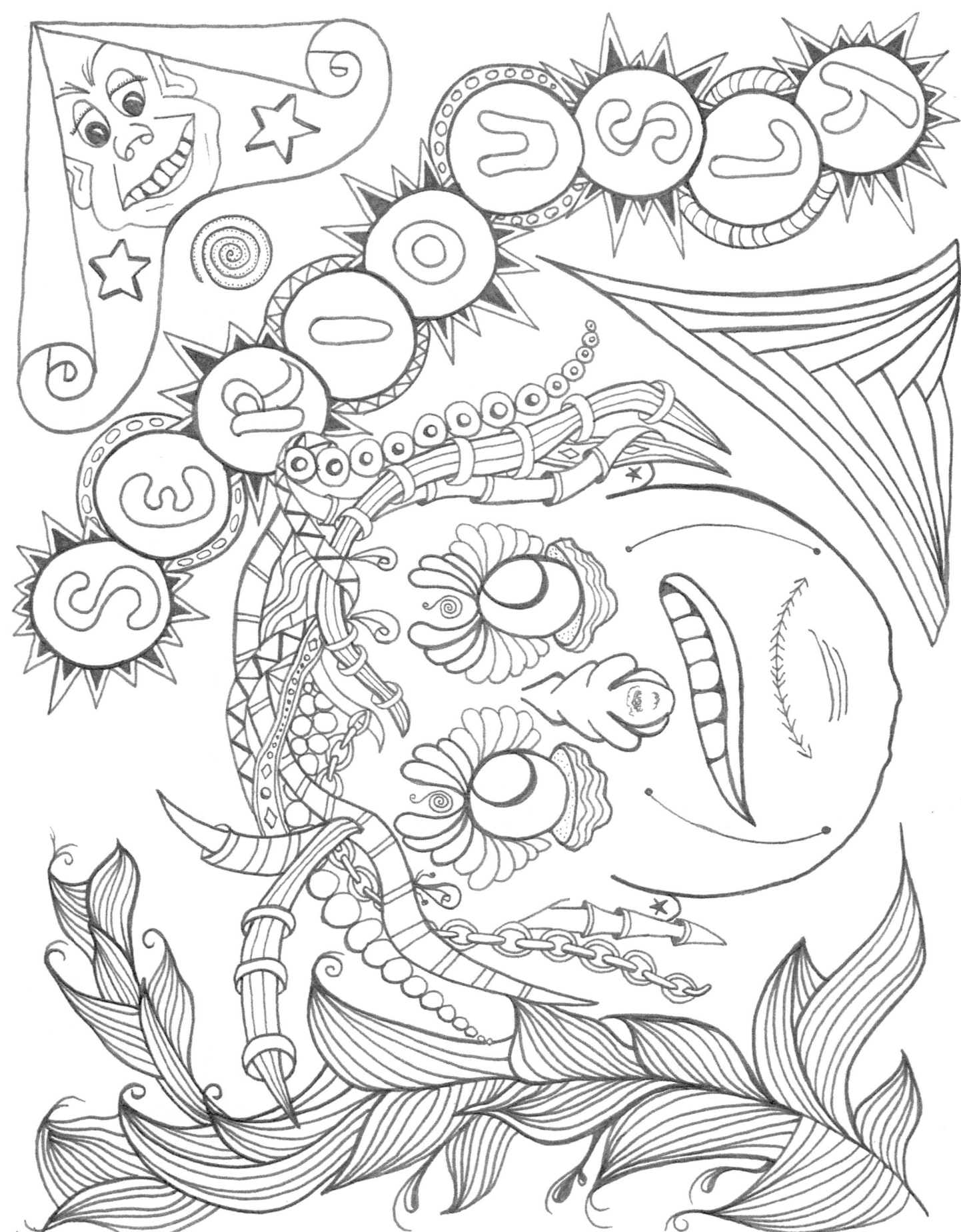

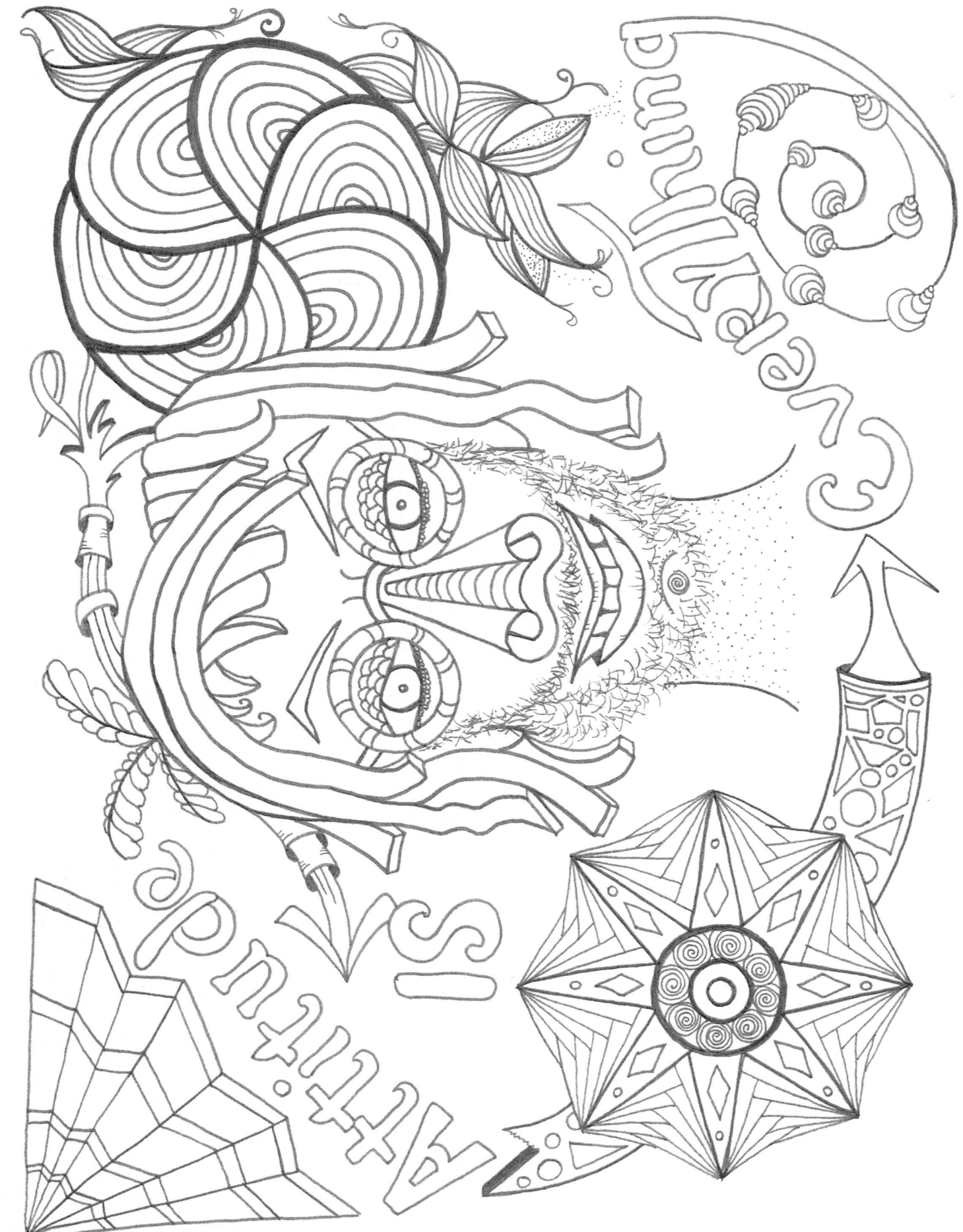

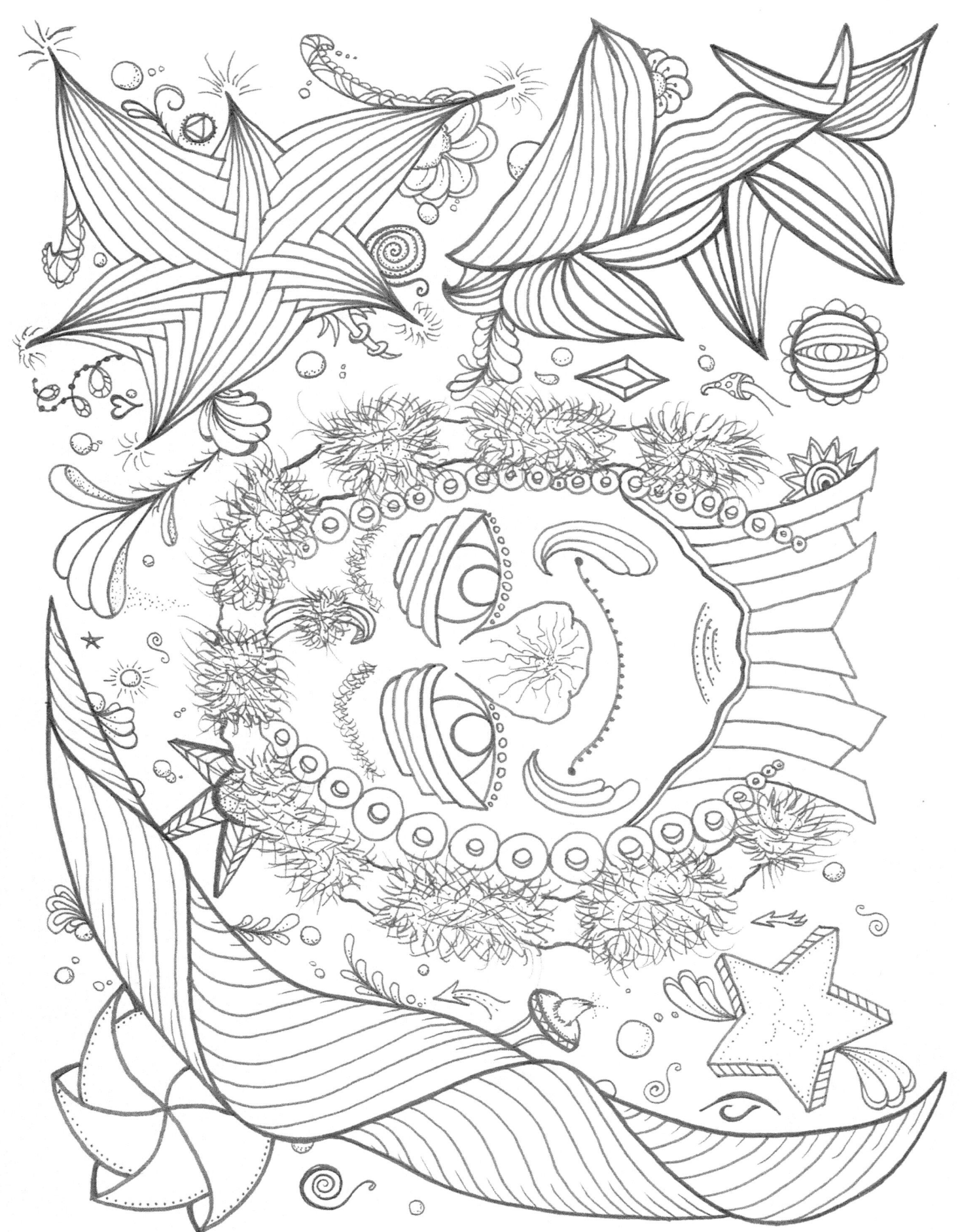

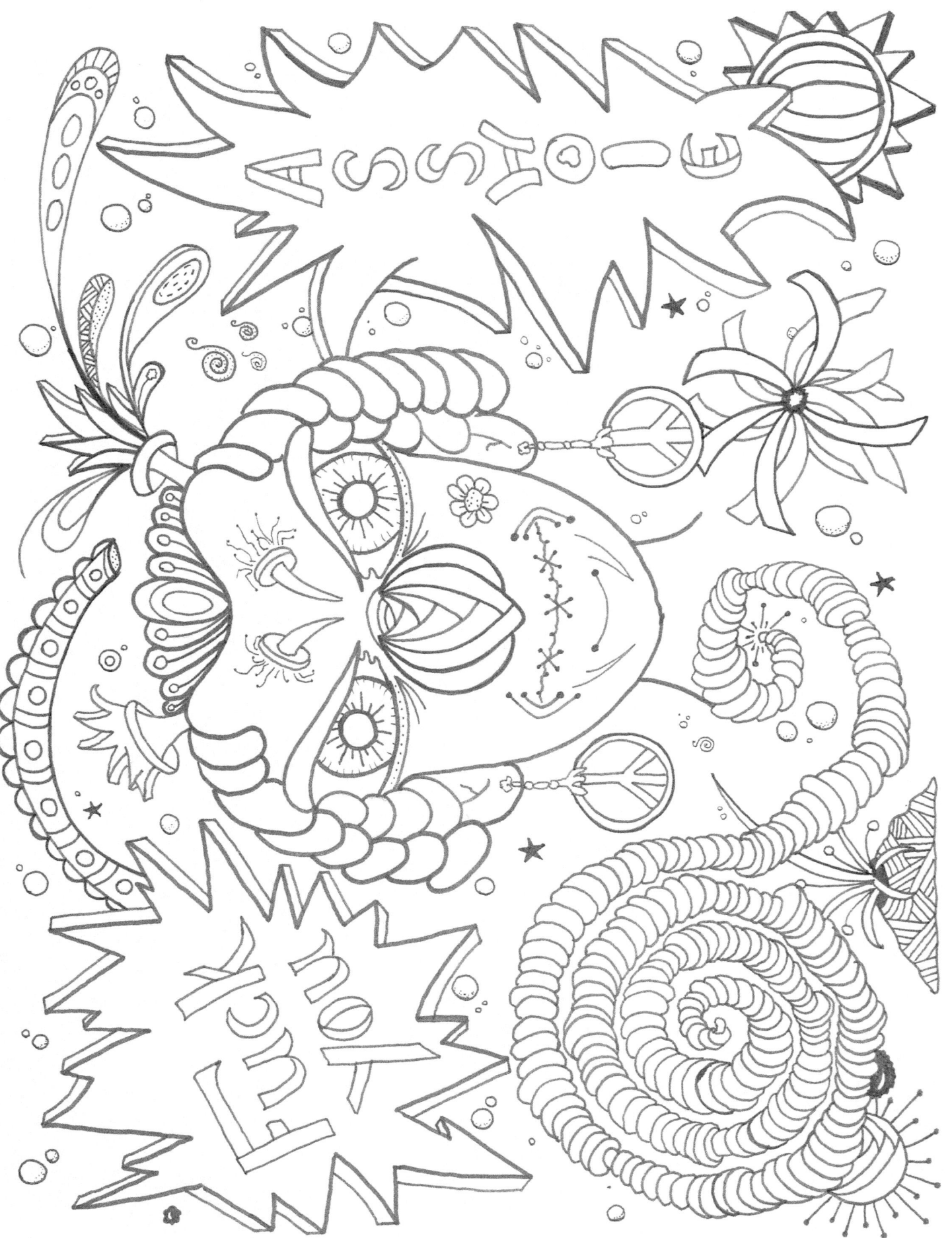

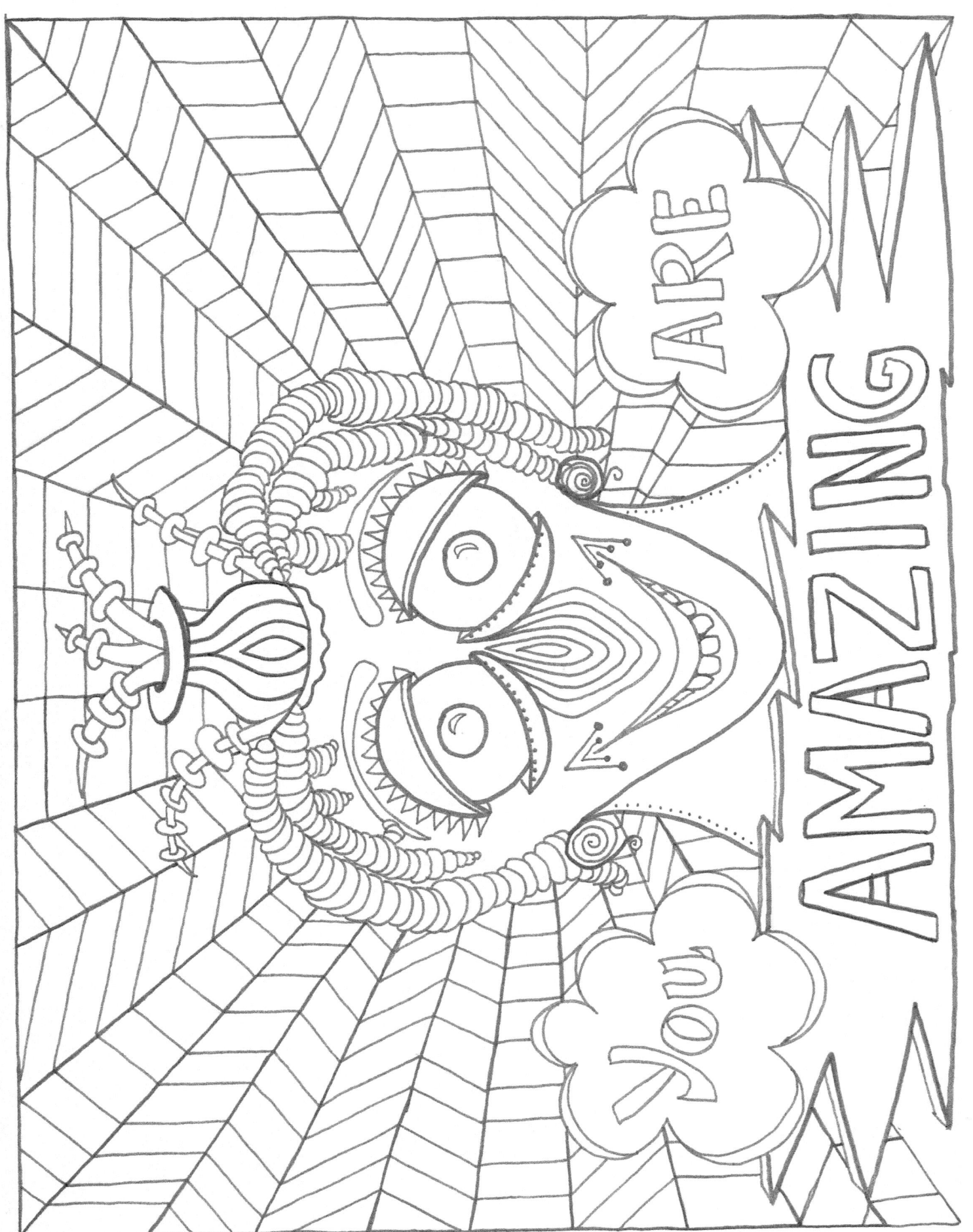

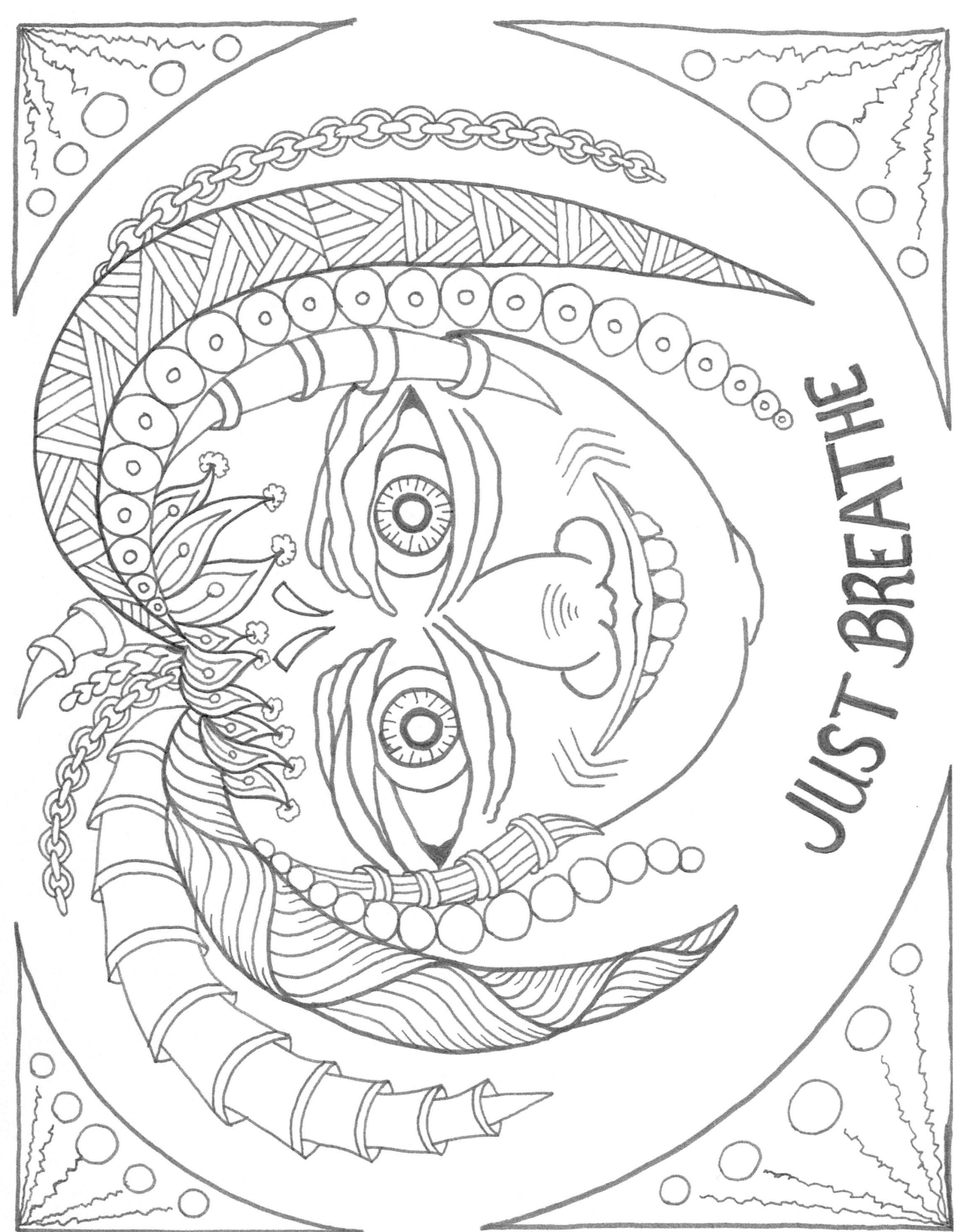

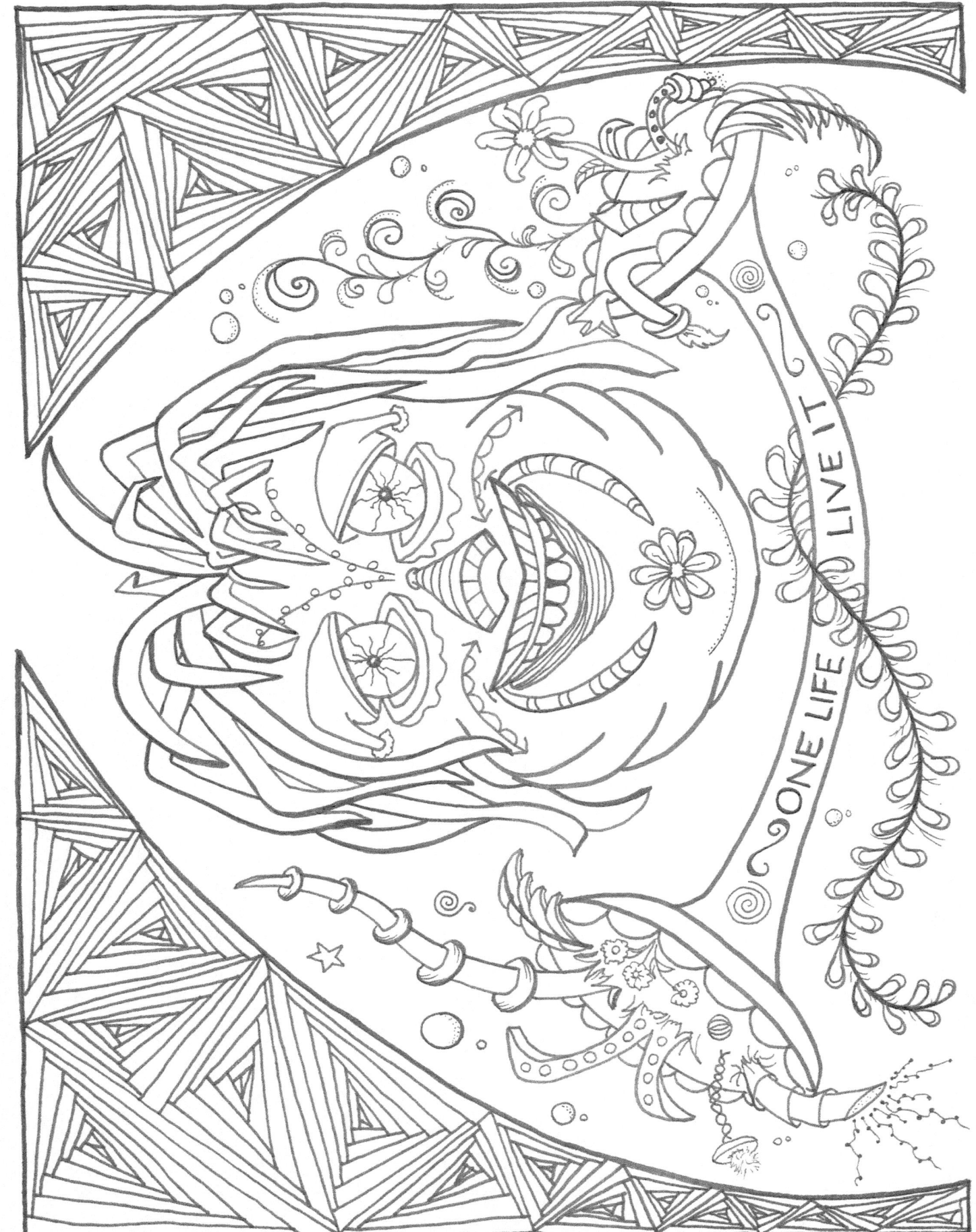

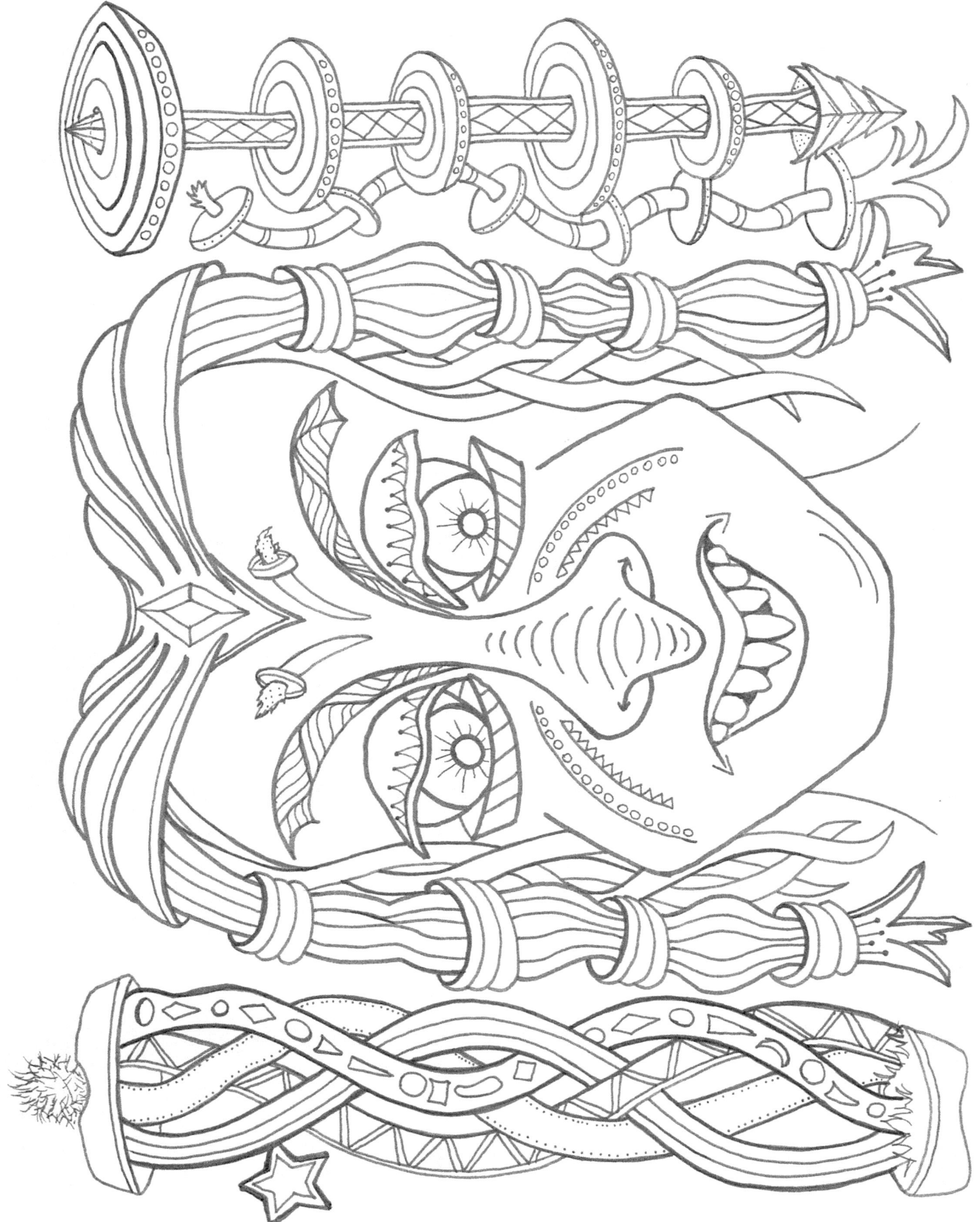

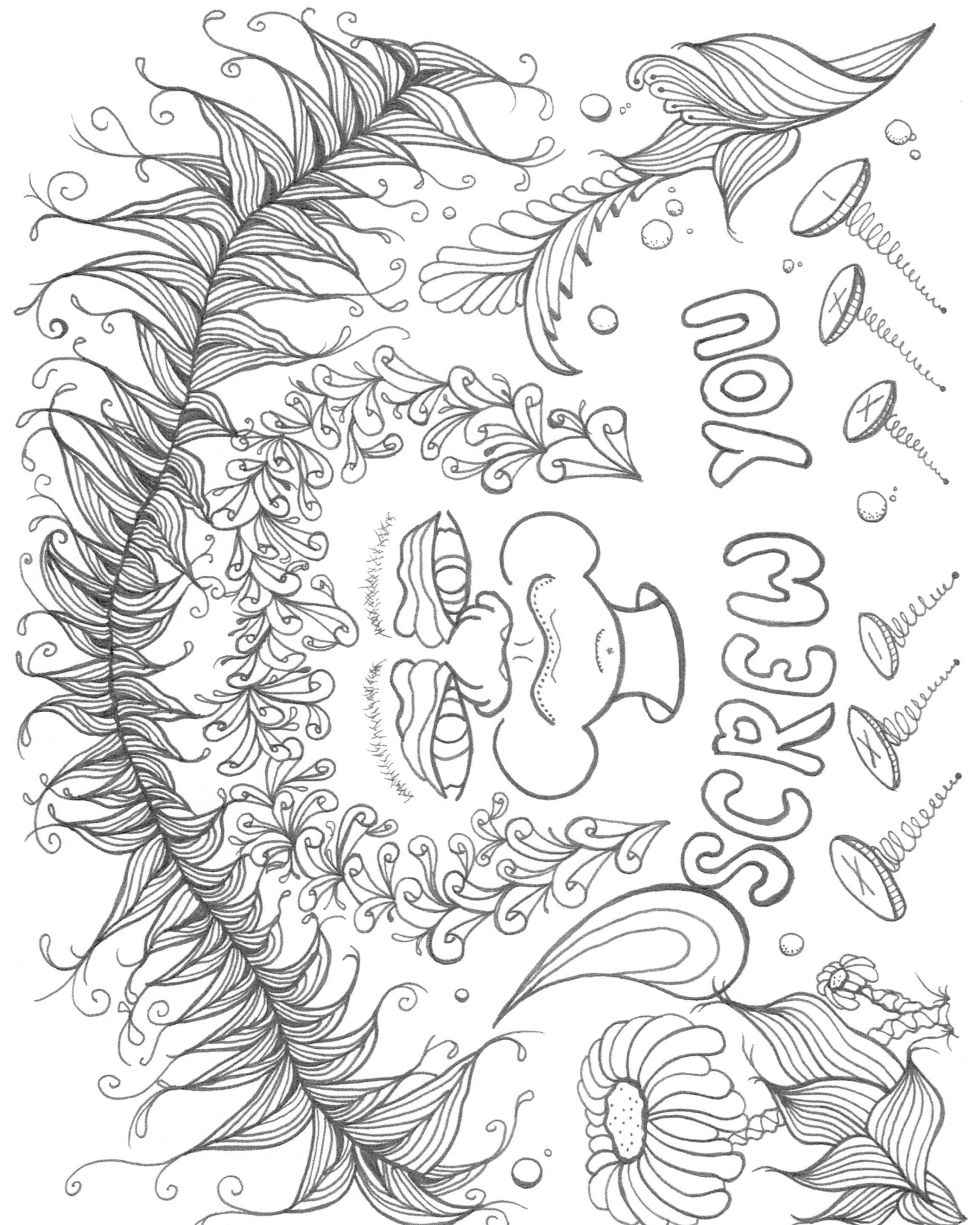

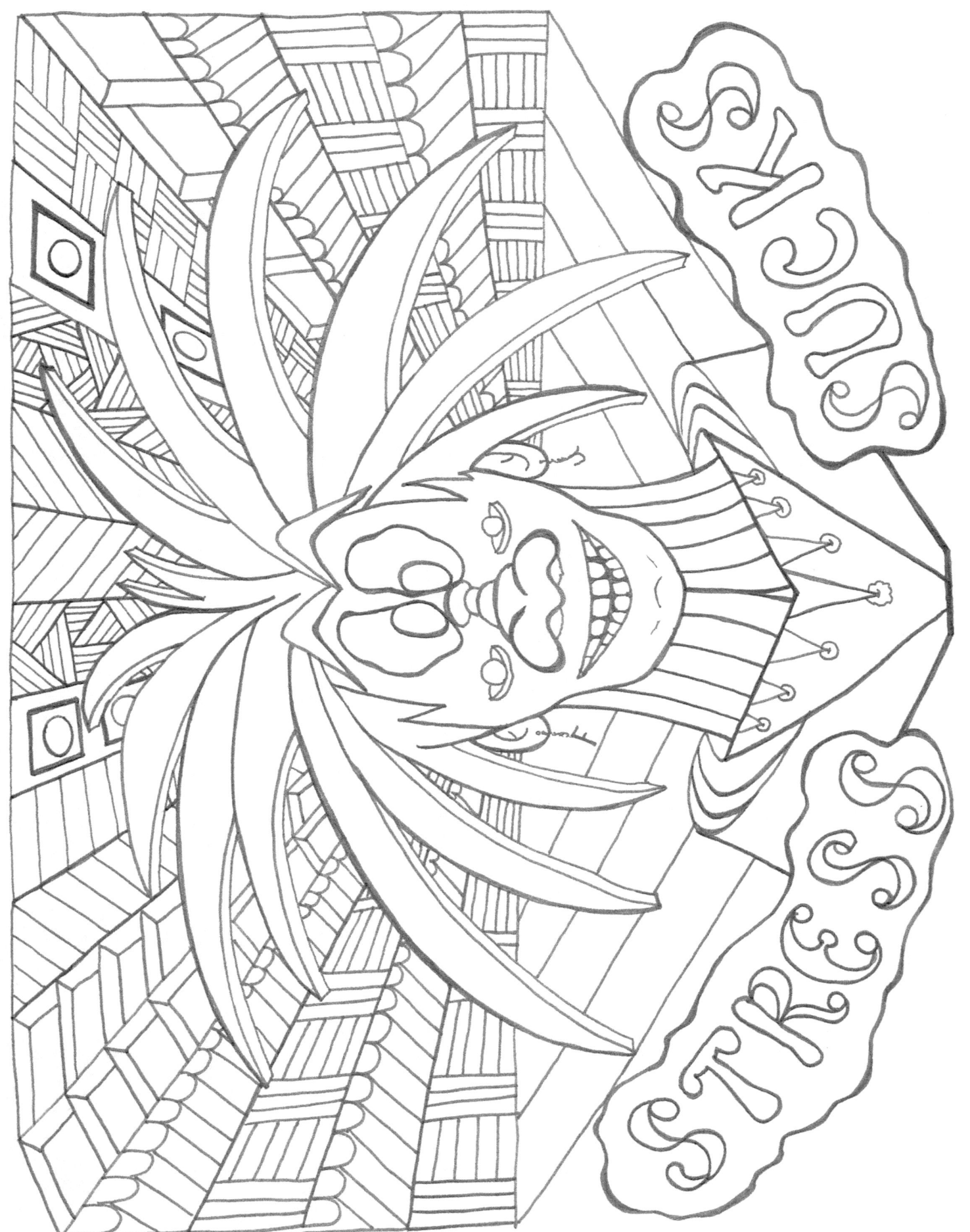